How to raise kids with autism

Brenda Bell

Table of Contents

INTRODUCTION

For many parents, raising a kid with autism offers a variety of ongoing difficulties. Although it must be noted right away that no two autistic children are the same, there are a number of realistic ways that can help on the journey of raising a child who is on the autism spectrum. The benefits may vary or not be felt at all in certain circumstances.

CHAPTER 1

Don't make comparisons

Making comparisons between your child and, for instance, his or her siblings who are not on the spectrum or with peers who are also not on the spectrum is not only pointless but also harmful for everyone involved.
Since no two autistic children exhibit the same traits or respond to various difficulties, in the same manner, even comparing your child to other autistic kids is pointless. Every child is different, so even though it might occasionally be difficult, try to think of your child's growth as his or her special adventure, one in which you will play a crucial part.

Social media has given us a 10,000-foot perspective into everybody's life, with guardians posting about their children's accomplishments, achievements, and festivities, and the sky is the limit from there. For any parent, the intuition to contrast their kids with others can be difficult to stand up to. Furthermore, for a parent of a kid with extraordinary requirements, it can bring one more degree of stress and nervousness into the overlap.
Comparison is normal and learning not to contrast your youngster with an inability with others requires exertion, however, it will get simpler with training and time unique necessities. While you'll continuously see contrasts between your kid and their average friends, you can prepare your brain not to zero in on that.

Realize it is normal to compare your child to others.
Allow guardians to contrast their children with different youngsters now and again, so it isn't something special to feel regretful about. Taking part in the way of behaving doesn't mean you don't cherish your kid, so offer yourself a reprieve. Just let it out's an exercise in futility.

Admit it's a waste of time
Contrasting two distinct individuals with each other will just prompt misery, pessimism, and a ton of stress. As guardians, as a rule, you ought to constantly remember this. When you help yourself to remember this, you'll before long end up doing it now and again and in the end, stop out and out. Every one of the enchanted lies in our discernment, Robinson says. "If you can see the positive characteristics in your kid, you'll normally quit contrasting him/her with anybody. Thus, you ought to attempt to search for no less than one new sure quality in your kid consistently."

Celebrate your child with special needs uniqueness.
Although it tends to be hard not to ponder the things your kid can't do, attempt to zero in on their assets and what makes them exceptional, "Their uniqueness will separate them as they progress in years, and they might try and have extraordinary capacities or abilities that they wouldn't in any case have."

Express your kid's assets.
There is a propensity to examine shortcomings as those things are contemplated, discussed, composed, printed, and discussed again in numerous gatherings. We should do the

same thing with qualities. On the off chance that there aren't many qualities recorded or expected in your gatherings, you'll need to do this part all alone. What's more, don't hesitate for even a moment to remind educators, managers, specialists, and specialists of every one of the magnificent things your youngster has achieved consistently.

It can likewise be useful to have your kids center around their capacities instead of their incapacities, particularly while they're feeling deterred by something. For 6 moves toward helping your kid (and you!) center around their capacities,

See the reality

Advise yourself that what you see from different kids is in many cases a feature reel similar to what we see via virtual entertainment, says Kathy Heath, Autism mindfulness advocate behind and mother of three kids, remembering one for the Autism range. Keep in mind, that no kid is awesome, and no parent has it simple.

Join a decent care group.

Find individual guardians of children with extraordinary necessities. They'll comprehend your battles and assist you with feeling like you're in good company,

Guardians will quite often see their future selves in their youngsters and for that reason, they maintain that they should be preferred in each field over them, at the end of the day, were. Along these lines, commonly they wind up pushing them excessively hard and contrasting them and their companions, and over-accomplishing neighbors' children or cousins. Notwithstanding, in the majority of the cases it leaves an unfriendly mental effect on the kids.

The following are a couple of basic practices which will assist guardians with disposing of this propensity.

Let yourself know that this isn't the way

Once in a while guardians make the ludicrous suspicion that continually pestering their children to coordinate with others will in some way or another increase their drive and potential, yet this is off-base. If it's not too much trouble, remember that how great your youngster turns out is exclusively, and exclusively your obligation.

Let yourself know that examination is off-base

Most importantly, you really should realize that different elements add to the improvement of a kid, and that incorporates his physical and mental capacity and his learning climate. If your youngster is experiencing issues getting a handle on illustrations or picking up something, converse with them and attempt to make it simpler
It could put you in a tough spot

No one enjoys being contrasted with others continually, and it's significantly more harmful and embarrassing when your folks are so cruel. You should comprehend that attracting steady correlations with others can make the kid feel that they are not adequate, and this can hurt their confidence, which is something you don't need. They could try and begin disdaining you.

Assemble shared trust

If your kids have zero faith in you, then you're a terrible parent. Making consistent correlations likewise makes you a terrible parent. To summarize the two, if you cause your kid to feel like they're a weight on you, they won't believe you and you'll have just yourself to a fault.

Figure out how to see the value in your youngster's uniqueness

Rather than continually attempting to cause your kid to copy the neighbor's child, it would be better if you begin considering your own kid's gifts. Praise them and award them assuming that they accomplish something pleasant.

Have tolerance

Figure out how to have persistence with your youngster and not push them excessively difficult to follow through with something, especially when they appear to be tracking down it troublesome or not looking into it.

CHAPTER 2

Help him /her recognize when they need a break

What is a Break?

A break is a chance for a kid to go to a pre-assigned spot either in a similar room or in an alternate space to quiet down, deal with tangible necessities, or as a prize for finishing prerequisites. One kid's break might appear to be unique from one more kid's contingent upon their particular necessities. A few youngsters will require many breaks, while others might require not very many. Occasionally a youngster might require more breaks while on different days less might be required. Breaks can be utilized really at school and home.

Who Needs a Break?

Most kids with an ASD require a break of some kind or another. Notwithstanding, some can self-direct and do fine with the regular breaks in a school day like breaks and a couple of moments of spare energy after finishing work. At home, a youngster who is self -controlled may naturally invest energy in their room without understanding that they are having some time off to stay away from unnecessary tactile feelings.

Numerous youngsters will require a greater number of breaks than this over their day and may not be aware to enjoy some time off all alone.

Typically this will prompt ways of behaving like work refusal; meandering around the room; leaving the study hall, everyday life; concealing under the work area; looking for tangible information like climbing or hopping on furnishings; shouting, or hollering; and tossing things around or becoming forceful.

Setting up a Break Area

Before carrying out a broken framework, have a particular region arranged that you believe the kid should use for breaks. If the motivation behind the break is to permit the kid to quiet down when upset, then have a tranquil region for the youngster to go to with negligible interruptions. If you are at home, a characteristic spot for a break is the kid's room. Ensure that there is nothing that could hurt in the room. Some of the time a kid will be irate and won't think plainly and will have no respect for their wellbeing. Additionally, make certain there is nothing flimsy in the room or region that could hurt.

Assuming the kid needs breaks to give explicit tangible information or to move away from a circumstance that is over-invigorating, then show the youngster a couple of things that are OK for the person in question to do. For instance, assuming the class is too uproarious the youngster might need to go to the library where it hushes up. You might need to send a clock with the kid so he knows when he ought to return. If at home, the youngster might be permitted to head outside and ride his bike on the porch for five minutes.

If the kid needs to move, have a taped-off region in the study hall or right external the entryway where the youngster realizes he can proceed to do bouncing jacks, the wall pushes, hopping, trusting, or lifting weighty items.

You might need to set up a board showing photos of different things the kid can do. For certain kids, you might need a CD player with earphones for the kid to pay attention to for a couple of moments. You may likewise need to have a break confine the region that is loaded up with tangible toys or other propelling things for the kid to play with.

Impart self-calming skills

Children frequently have meltdowns, but it can be challenging to calm an autistic youngster. Some autistic kids can pick up self-calming skills to use when they start to feel out of control of themselves or their environment.

CHAPTER 3

Discipline Strategies for children with Autism

At the point when a kid gets out of hand, whether the tricky way of behaving is pitching an attitude fit, hitting another youngster, or overlooking guidelines, you might be learned to reprimand them or remove specific honors. Be that as it may, training a youngster with Autism might require an alternate methodology

Conventional discipline procedures aren't generally compelling for a kid with Autism. Contingent upon where they fall on the range, they could battle to figure out results or handle unforgiving censures. Yet, that doesn't mean you shouldn't utilize any discipline whatsoever. All things considered, gentler and more reliable techniques might be the way to assist kids with Autism deal with their way of behaving.

Grasping Common Autistic Behaviors

We typically discipline youngsters since they deliberately act in unseemly ways, whether it's swiping treats off a kin's plate or purposefully stumbling a kid on the soccer field. In any case, a kid with Autism will most likely be unable to control specific ways of behaving, and they mustn't be brutally rebuffed for them.

Ways of behaving that youngsters with Autism might battle to control include:

- Gnawing their hands and fingers
- Hand fluttering or shaking (a self-invigorating way of behaving that assists individuals with Autism manage their feelings)
- Shouting or hollering
- Harming themselves by banging or hitting their heads
- Not taking a gander at individuals or visually connecting
- Actual hostility toward peers and adults, such as gnawing or kicking.

A significant number of these ways of behaving stem from kids' battles to communicate their necessities or wants or figure out normal practices and cues. You shouldn't put your kid in the break, disgrace them, or hit them due to these ways of behaving. Rather, it's significant that you work to more readily comprehend the reason why they are carrying on along these lines and, if essential, attempt to stay away from those triggers from here on out.

What Is Gentle Discipline?

Utilize Positive Reinforcement

Youngsters with Autism answer better to train procedures that emphasize the positive. With uplifting feedback systems, you point out things your kid is doing well (involving their calm voice in the grocery store, for instance) and commend them or prize them for it.

A few kids may be persuaded by an exemplary sticker outline, where they can gather stickers for a good way of behaving and at last procure an award for a specific number of stickers. In any case, numerous kids with Autism, especially youthful ones, answer criticism and prizes that relate straightforwardly to the way of behaving. For instance, if they ask pleasantly for a plush toy in a store as opposed to shouting or hitting their heads in dissatisfaction, they procure prompt recognition (and perhaps, if suitable, the toy).

One straightforward self-quieting method they can attempt is to take in and out through their nose gradually while shutting their eyes and envisioning something charming, similar to their kitty or their number one park. Assuming you or one more believed a grown-up is near, they can embrace the grown-up until they're settled. Delicate, consistent tension, as from an embrace, is quieting for some kids with autism.

Control Their Environment

For kids with Autism particularly, it's useful to make their prompt climate helpful for their solace. Taking consideration filling their play region or room with favored toys and articles can cause them to have a good sense of security and agreeableness, which might prompt more controlled behavior.

Alternately, attempt to keep away from circumstances that you know can set off their unsettling — for certain children with Autism, for instance, it may very well be packed or loud puts — and be watching out for indications of forthcoming disappointment.

Here and there, jokes with Autism can be enthusiastic about certain toys or exercises and that can slow down essential routines. These interruptions can be eliminated when errands should be finished.

Stick to Routines

Many children with Autism ache for consistency and request and can battle to adapt when normal schedules are disrupted. They could blow up or increment self-invigorating ways of behaving to manage capricious circumstances. Assist them by restricting the number of exercises you have with having them do and adhering to an anticipated timetable.

That could mean skirting a language training meeting multi-week as opposed to knocking it to one more day when the educator is coincidentally twofold reserved or making an effort not to fit in unexpected, startling tasks with them following some serious time at school. Make a timetable that you can show in your kid's room or a typical region with pictures they can use to rapidly distinguish what they can hope to do every day of the week (like a photograph of their language teacher on Tuesday).

Convey Clearly

It's ideal to utilize plain language and orders with kids who have Autism. Kids with Autism range problems frequently experience difficulty figuring out nuances in verbal language or non-verbal communication.

At the point when your kid begins carrying on, direct them to what you favor them to do instead of what they shouldn't do. For instance, if a kid is pulling a canine's tail, don't say, "Quit harming the canine." Instead, you can say, "Pet the canine delicately."

Overlook Harmless Behaviors
A few ways of behaving of youngsters with Autism appear to be bizarre however aren't hazardous or problematic. Essential instances of this are self-animating ways of behaving like hand-fluttering or shaking.
If issue conduct happens rarely, doesn't keep your family or others from normal schedules, and doesn't hurt your youngster or others, then it ought to be disregarded at whatever point possible.

Put Safety First
Numerous youngsters with Autism don't show conduct that would hurt themselves or others. Notwithstanding, at whatever point you are managing a circumstance wherein a kid is truly erupting, you want to ensure that they (and others around them) are protected.
Assuming that your youngster is having a fit of rage that is difficult to stop, make certain to eliminate hard or sharp items that may be in their way. If you are experiencing difficulty eliminating your kid from a populated spot, (for example, the jungle gym or a birthday celebration), enlist help from one more adult to occupy and guide different youngsters to another area.

Look for Professional Help
Assuming that you are finding it hard to deal with your kid's way of behaving, make it a point to proficient assistance. Search for individuals with aptitude in assisting kids with Autism, as formative conduct pediatricians or kid therapists.

There are a few treatments that are useful for youngsters with Autism. Most originate from the standards of applied conduct investigation (ABA), which centers around building and empowering new abilities, giving admittance to favored exercises and toys, giving children decisions while conceivable, expanding suitable correspondence, and making complex circumstances more unsurprising utilizing signals and other routine gestures.

For what reason do kids with Autism require rules and discipline?

Limits are vital to living in the public eye, regardless of your neurological cosmetics. Like all kids — yet maybe to a more noteworthy degree than most — youngsters with Autism regularly flourish with a schedule. Laying out rules and cutoff points is an approach to building up schedules, which might be a solace to messing with Autism.

Stick to Routines

At the point when a kid makes trouble, whether the dangerous way of behaving is pitching an attitude fit, hitting another youngster, or overlooking directions, you might be taught to reprimand them or remove specific honors. Yet, training a youngster with Autism might require an alternate methodology.

Customary discipline methods aren't generally compelling for a kid with Autism.

Contingent upon where they fall on the range, they could battle to grasp results or handle cruel censures. Yet, that doesn't mean you shouldn't utilize any discipline whatsoever. All things being equal, gentler and steady procedures might be the way to assist youngsters with Autism and deal with their way of behaving.

The most effective method to Manage Misbehavior Without Punishment

Figuring out Common Autistic Behaviours

We generally discipline kids since they deliberately act in unseemly ways, whether it's swiping treats off a kin's plate or purposefully stumbling a kid on the soccer field. In any case, a kid with a Autism will most likely be unable to control specific ways of behaving, and they mustn't be cruelly rebuffed for them. A way of behaving that kids with Autism might battle to control include:

- Gnawing their hands and fingers
- Hand fluttering or shaking (a self-invigorating way of behaving that assists individuals withAutism control their feelings)
- Shouting or hollering
- Harming themselves by banging or hitting their heads
- Not taking a gander at individuals or visually connecting
- Actual animosity toward peers and adults, such as gnawing or kicking

Large numbers of these ways of behaving stem from kids' battles to communicate their requirements or wants or figure out normal practices and prompts. You shouldn't put your kid on break, disgrace them, or beat them on account of these ways of behaving. Rather, it's significant you work to all the more likely comprehend the reason why they are carrying on along these lines and, if vital, attempt to keep away from those triggers from here on out.

CHAPTER 4

Keep an open mind

Aside from the clinical consideration and treatments that you might arrange to help your child or girl, there are straightforward, regular things that have an effect;

- Center around the positive: Very much like any other person, kids with mental Autism range jumble frequently answer well to uplifting feedback. That implies when you acclaim them for the ways of behaving they're getting along admirably, it will make them (and you) feel much better.
- Be explicit, with the goal that they know precisely exact thing you loved about their way of behaving. Track down ways of remunerating them, either with additional recess or a little award like a sticker.
- Likewise, as you would with anybody on the range or not prize your kid for what their identity is. As a parent, cherishing your kid for what their identity is vital.
- Remain reliable and on time: Individuals on the range like schedules. Ensure they get reliable direction and cooperation, so they can rehearse what they gain from treatment. This can make acquiring new abilities and ways of behaving more straightforward, and assist them with applying their insight in various circumstances. Converse with their instructors and specialists and attempt to adjust on a reliable arrangement of procedures and techniques for

cooperation so you can bring what they're realizing home.

- Put play on the timetable: Finding exercises that seem like unadulterated tomfoolery, and not more schooling or treatment, may help your kid open up and associate with you.

- Give now is the right time: You'll probably attempt various procedures, medicines, and approaches as you sort out what's best for your kid. Remain positive and make an effort not to get deterred on the off chance that they don't answer well to a specific technique.

- Take your youngster along for regular exercises: In the event that your kid's way of behaving is eccentric, you might feel like presenting them to specific situations is more straightforward not. However, when you take them on regular tasks like shopping for food or a mailing station run, it might assist them with getting them used to their general surroundings.

- Get support: Whether on the web or eye to eye, support from different families, experts, and companions can be a major assistance. Make a town of loved ones who figure out your youngster's determination. Companionships might be troublesome, and your youngster will require support in keeping up with those kinships.

  Support gatherings can be an effective method for sharing exhortation and data and to meet different guardians managing comparative difficulties. Individual, conjugal, or family guiding can be useful, as well. Ponder what could make your life somewhat simpler, and request help.

- Investigate reprieve care: This is the point at which another guardian cares for your kid inside your home, beyond it, or both for a while to offer you a short reprieve. You'll require it, particularly assuming that your kid has extreme necessities because of ASD. This can allow you an opportunity to do things that reestablish your own wellbeing and that you appreciate, so you return home prepared to help.

You can recognize or shape your relief support group utilizing these strategies:

- Ask your companions, family, and different guardians you know for help associations you probably won't have contemplated.

- Check with your kid's primary care physicians, advisors, and educators for thoughts or references. For example, a student teacher you truly like could appreciate minding their leisure time.

- You can likewise post sees for childcare help in papers and on the web, neighborhood strict networks, and at schools and colleges close to you. Make certain to painstakingly take a look at all references.

- Join a care group for guardians of Autism youngsters. Figure out what works for other people. You can find self improvement networks by calling a nearbyAutism support focus or looking on the web.

- Deal with yourself: As a parental figure, you really want to keep your body and your psyche in excellent condition so you can confront the difficulties that harvest up from one day to another. This implies dialing back and searching for ways of dealing with yourself so you'll have a lot of you (genuinely, intellectually, and inwardly) to go around.

- Cut your pressure: Guardians of children with ASD frequently face more pressure than the people who manage different incapacities. Whenever left unrestrained, guardians can confront breakdowns in connections and, surprisingly, mental issues. Stress can influence your wellbeing, as well. Remain coordinated to assist yourself with trying not to get overpowered. This implies carving out opportunity in your day only for yourself.

A significant and, surprisingly, fun ways of doing that include:

1. Pinpoint the genuine reasons for your pressure: Assuming you feel overpowered, separate the significant issues you're looking into simpler nibbles. You'll feel improved, and you'll have an arrangement.

2. Reflection might help, as well: Focus on your viewpoints and the manner in which you converse with yourself. It'll help you get rid of pointless concerns.

3. Work out: You don't have to go to the rec center. Walk, work in the nursery, swim, even dance in the kitchen. These are simple, compelling ways of getting some activity. On the off chance that you need some grown-up organization, take an activity class. It's an extraordinary method for re-energizing your batteries and meet new individuals.

4. Get some Sleep: At the point when you really want to re-energize your body and psyche, you can't beat the force of a decent night's rest. In the event that you really want additional assistance slowing down, ponder or do unwinding works out. That can assist your body with preparing for rest.

5. Get inventive with your food: You probably burn through loads of effort ensuring your kid eats nutritious feasts. And you? Brighten up your own menu by attempting various natural products, veggies, and cooking styles. Really take a look at new recipes to keep things fascinating. What's more, eat on a set timetable every day. It'll assist you with keeping your energy up and your framework on target.

6. Get balance in your life: This is the key not exclusively to confronting life's difficulties, yet

additionally keeping a great of life. Your entire family will benefit. Book time in your week after week schedule for entertainment only and mingling.

Attempt these tips to add equilibrium to your bustling days:

- Track down your companions: Indeed, you're the parent of an exceptional necessities youngster. In any case, you're an individual, as well. Recollecting that you have your own character makes you a superior parent. Find opportunity to reconnect and snicker with your companions. You'll be happy you did.

- Take up old leisure activities: Find your sewing needles, dust off the piano, or get out the golf clubs. Attempt new exercises that get your attention.

- Require five consistently: A couple of additional minutes first thing can focus you and set the vibe for the entire day. Assemble your contemplations, take a long, warm shower, or scribble a few notes in a diary.

- Hurry up: Could your accomplice or other relatives at any point take over a little? A speedy stroll around the block or short drive to the store without anyone else, will give you a truly necessary opportunity to yourself.you want to keep your body and your psyche in excellent condition so you can confront the difficulties that harvest up from one day to another.

This implies dialing back and searching for ways of dealing with yourself so you'll have a lot of you (genuinely, intellectually, and inwardly) to go around.

- Cut your pressure: Guardians of children with ASD frequently face more pressure than the people who manage different incapacities.
  Whenever left unrestrained, guardians can confront breakdowns in connections and, surprisingly, mental issues. Stress can influence your well-being, as well. Remain coordinated to assist yourself with trying not to get overpowered. This implies carving out opportunities in your day only for yourself.

CHAPTER 5

Maintain a sense of humour

The vast majority mean well when they attempt to remember Autism people for their social associations and discussions. Nonetheless, in some cases, they may accidentally say or do things that cause them to notice the Autism individual's spasms and cause humiliation.

Here are a few hints on the most proficient method to best remember kids for the range so they feel invited:

- Take an opportunity to find out about Autism: If you don't know how to collaborate with Autism individual, it's alright to inquire. Additionally, there are incredible assets to find out about Autism on the web, where you can find out about more normal side effects like tangible over-burden and summed-up tension. Finding out about Autism will make it simpler to sympathize with the companion you're attempting to incorporate.

- Treat messes around with Autism in the manner in which you would treat some other youngster: Remembering them for exercises with others their age will assist them with their socialization abilities. Likewise, while addressing a youngster with Autism, many tragically have an erroneously over-energetic manner of speaking. This can appear to be annoying and distant to the person.

- Accept what makes them unique: Try not to respond or cause to notice their murmurs, spasms, or folds. That is a piece of what their identity is. Pointing out these things that make him different may humiliate them and make them more averse to connecting.

- Kids appreciate jumping hands first into play encounters: Getting done with the responsibilities of building blocks, working on a riddle, and drawing pictures will yield abilities that the youngster will use all through his lifetime.

Specialists who work with youngsters are specialists in taking a gander at various games, exercises, and toys to figure out which abilities a kid needs to finish them. It is a tomfoolery task to have for sure!
Recollect that kids are wired to utilize their faculties to foster abilities during play.
Toys that can be utilized in numerous ways and that includes more than one sense will naturally be more charming. Multi-tactile implies that more pathways to mental health are opened and utilized.

10 THERAPEUTIC ACTIVITIES FOR CHILDREN WITH AUTISM

1) POOL NOODLES

One of the least expensive and most flexible bits of gear to suggest is a straightforward froth pool noodle. They can be utilized in countless ways. Stock up at your neighborhood secondhand shop in the spring and summer for all-year fun.

Here are far to utilize them:

- Pool noodle treatment toys pool noodle toys for Autism
- Cut them up into two-inch parts of the stack and construct like blocks
- Name bits of pool noodles with each letter of the letters in order and stack bits of pool noodles on top of one another in sequential request
- Make boats out of pool noodles, straws, and triangles
- Use straws, pipe cleaners, and googly eyes to make bugs
- String two-inch bits of pool noodles utilizing a piece of string or rope
- Slice them down the middle upward and make pathways for water play
- Make hindrance courses out of pool noodles cut down the middle to make balance radiates
- Make light sabers out of pool noodles by cutting them into quarters and wrapping channel tape around the highest point of each quarter to make a handle.

2) CREATE SENSORY BINS FULL OF FUN ITEMS

It's so natural to get stuck utilizing just rice or grain. To forestall an enormous wreck, play on top of a shower drapery.

- Aquarium rock comes in amazing varieties
- Easter grass
- straws cut up into pieces, as a matter of fact, let kids slice the straws to construct fine coordinated movements
- feathers

- moon batter
- tissue paper pieces
- strip
- fastens and dabs
- soil and sand

3) CREATE A SAFE SENSORY TIME-OUT AREA

The region ought to be in a spot in which your youngster has a good sense of reassurance and can unwind, so try not to make it in that frame of mind of the family's home. Urge your kid to work with you and give them decisions on material and what goes in the tangible region.

Assuming that you are feeling aggressive, you could make your kid a whole tangible room.

Utilize an enormous cardboard box from a machine and tape the edges with hued pipe tape to forestall paper cuts.

Hang a hula loop beautified with strips so they overflow down. This is a marvelous visual looking like a brilliant cascade which is magnificent for material play as well!

Indeed, even a storeroom or corner can work. It's inside that is significant.

Add a CD player or music your kid tracks down quieting.

Ensure your youngster has squirm things to keep hands occupied.

4) SENSORY SWINGS FOR AUTISM

Swinging is an exceptionally restorative action for youngsters with Autism! There are countless various ways of involving a swing for treatment.

They are flexible in that they can be utilized for quieting and self-guideline, or simply a tomfoolery, pleasant movement!

5) VISUAL SCHEDULES

Visual timetables have been basic in both my facility and in my own home. I rely upon a schedule and timetable to stay focused. It's been demonstrated that numerous kids with Autism are visual students. This implies that an image plan illustrating the means of an undertaking is useful.

In any event, for day-to-day errands, for example, cleaning up, a timetable of the means ought to be posted so that children know the precisely exact thing to expect and what comes straightaway. This can be integrated into play exercises. In this way, take photos of a block pinnacle and number them.

Request that your youngster set up them by getting out, Whatever starts things out, etc. Perhaps the most supportive device guardians can utilize is a camera. Make stride-by-step photographs of every movement, print, and cover them.

6) MAKE AN OBSTACLE COURSE

Use anything you can find. Taped lines are superb for 'imagine' balance radiates. Hula circles, bean pack throwing, and hop ropes can be in every way included. Strolling like creatures is consistently tomfoolery and fabricate wonderful gross coordinated abilities.

- bounce like a frog
- dash like a pony
- crawl like a snake
- creep like a little dog
- squirm like a worm
- bounce like a kangaroo

- walk like a crab
- skip like a unicorn

7) SENSORY AND CALM-DOWN BOTTLES
tactile jug The option of more modest things your youngster leans towards making the containers tomfoolery and add visual allure. For instance, add hair gel with a touch of water and sparkle so the sparkle falls gradually through the jug. Paper cuts are enjoyable to add so that children can utilize a magnet to draw in and move the paper cuts all through the container.

These are the fury at present. Why? They can be modified for every kid and are intended for some reasons. They can be made with water, hair gel, water dots, and other filler materials.

8) PLAYGROUND AND OUTDOOR ACTIVITIES
Autism kid outside inquiries concerning why he doesn't lean toward the gear or just strolls around and around the jungle gym as opposed to involving the hardware as planned. Offer fun choices, for example, alphabetic scrounger chases and finding things starting with each letter of the letters in order. These kinds of exercises assist youngsters with utilizing such countless faculties together. Urge children to play outside and in uncovered feet whenever the situation allows. On the off chance that your kid isn't enamored with jungle gym hardware, he might be telling you that he wants extra treatment to conquer a trepidation or engine shortcoming.

9) INVOLVE YOUR CHILD IN DAILY DECISIONS
Recollect that youngsters love to take part and gain parental endorsement. Indeed, even most everyday assignments can be fun when done together. For instance, set a week-after-week menu. Glance through cookbooks and the storage room to conclude what things should be added to the staple rundown. Ask your youngster what feasts he likes and request that he figure out the necessary things and keep in touch with them on the rundown. Then, at that point, shop together and work on getting to know the store. At long last, looking at assists with cash the board and planning. Recollect that a definitive objective is for your kid to work freely and it's never past the point where it is possible to begin.

10) ADD 'Mind BREAKS' OR YOGA AND MOVEMENT ACTIVITIES
These can be integrated all through your kid's day. It's basic to guarantee your kid is enjoying some time off at school and getting ready intellectually for troublesome tasks and tests.

Profound breathing and quieting systems ought to be drilled when things are quiet and not upsetting so they can be effectively gotten to when a kid is worried.

CHAPTER 6

Look into Applied Behavioral Analysis (ABA) therapy.

What is Applied Behavior Analysis (ABA)?
Applied Behavior Analysis (ABA) is a way to deal with understanding and evolving conduct. It's anything but a particular treatment itself, however a scope of various procedures and strategies that can be utilized to assist medically introverted individuals with mastering new abilities and conduct.
At the point when ABA procedures are utilized with youthful medically introverted kids, it's not unexpected called Early Intensive Behavioral Intervention (EIBI).

Who is Applied Behavior Analysis (ABA) for?
Applied Behavior Analysis (ABA) shows procedures can be utilized for Autism youngsters and kids with other formative handicaps.

What is Applied Behavior Analysis (ABA) utilized for?
The Applied Behavior Analysis (ABA) approach and its procedures can assist Autism youngsters with working on their interactive abilities, taking care of themselves abilities, relational abilities, play abilities, and capacity to deal with their way of behaving. It can likewise assist with diminishing conduct like distractedness, animosity, and shouting.

ABA can assist Autism youngsters with creating autonomy, however, it ought not to be utilized to make kids 'veil' their autism or 'fit in' with accepted practices.

Where does Applied Behavior Analysis (ABA) come from?

Applied Behavior Analysis (ABA) depends on the learning hypothesis, which comes from the field of social brain research. The principal concentration that took a gander at the utilization of ABA strategies with youthful Autism youngsters was distributed by Dr. Ivar Lovaas at the University of California at Los Angeles (UCLA) in 1987. There was a long-haul follow-up concentrate by Dr. John McEachin at UCLA, which was distributed in 1993.

What is the thought behind Applied Behavior Analysis (ABA) for Autism kids?

These are the vital thoughts behind Applied Behavior Analysis (ABA):

- The human way of behaving is impacted by occasions or upgrades in the climate.
- Conduct that is trailed by sure outcomes is bound to reoccur.
- ABA utilizes these plans to assist Autism youngsters with learning a new way of behaving. It does this by giving kids positive ramifications for a new way of behaving. For instance, if a youngster focuses on a teddy they need, the kid's folks could follow this up with a positive outcome like giving the kid the teddy. This makes it more probable that the youngster will rehash the conduct from now on.

What does Applied Behavior Analysis (ABA) for Autism kids include?

Programs because of Applied Behavior Analysis (ABA) by and large include:

- Evaluating a youngster's ongoing abilities and troubles.
- Defining objectives and targets - for instance, figuring out how to make proper acquaintance.
- Planning and carrying out a program that shows the 'target' expertise
- Estimating the 'target' ability to see whether the program is working
- Assessing the actual program and making changes on a case-by-case basis.

- ABA can zero in on a particular way of behaving, such as over and over taking off safety belts in the vehicle, or it can work all the more extensively on a scope of formative regions simultaneously, similar to correspondence, taking care of oneself and play abilities.

- ABA programs utilize a scope of training procedures to assist Autism kids with mastering new abilities. These procedures could incorporate Discrete Trial Training and accidental instructing. Projects could likewise involve regular collaborations as any open doors for kids to learn.

- Youngsters are offered a lot of chances to rehearse new abilities. As they acquire abilities, more abilities are added to their projects. Over the long haul, abilities are joined into complex ways of behaving, such as having discussions, playing agreeably with others, or advancing by watching others.

- Contingent upon their necessities, youngsters can do ABA programs in a balanced or little gathering design at a middle, at home, or locally.

- There are various styles of ABA, going from exceptionally organized and unbending to more adaptable. There are marked projects that utilize ABA standards, including the Lovaas Program. Furthermore, there are different projects in light of the standards of ABA, including Early Intensive Behavioral Intervention (EIBI).

- ABA programs for youthful medically introverted kids as a rule include over 20 hours of treatment each week. Research has shown that this power is how ABA programs accomplish results.

- ABA projects ought to perceive Autism kids' on the whole correct to stim or move in actually agreeable manners. They ought to include leisure time, loosening up exercises, and open doors for youngsters to have their feelings met. ABA programs shouldn't include discipline.

Does Applied Behavior Analysis (ABA) help medically introverted youngsters?

Applied Behavior Analysis (ABA) is a successful methodology for showing a scope of abilities to Autism youngsters. Quality examination demonstrates the way that it can decidedly affect medically introverted kids' correspondence, mental, and conduct abilities.
Given the variety in how ABA is applied, be that as it may, you could have to look at the results of explicit projects to decide whether they're ideal for your kid.

Applied Behavior Analysis (ABA): concerns and debate
Quality exploration shows that Applied Behavior Analysis (ABA) can assist medically introverted kids with acquiring new abilities and conduct.

However, there are a few worries and discussions about ABA:
A few Autism individuals say that ABA depends on the possibility that medically introverted kids ought to act equivalent to normally creating youngsters. They say that this thought doesn't regard neurodiversity. That is, it doesn't acknowledge and regard regular contrasts in how individuals' cerebrums work and how they comprehend and communicate with the world.

- A few Autism individuals feel that ABA programs once in a while mean to stop conduct like fluttering or stimming, which can be quieting or pleasant for Autism individuals.

- ABA projects can include numerous long periods of redundant, coordinated treatment every day and week. This power is a fundamental part of ABA, however, it very well may be a worry for youngsters.

- A few Autism individuals say ABA is destructive because it doesn't put medically introverted youngsters' prosperity first.

- Previously, ABA programs utilized discipline to quit testing conduct, albeit this is by all accounts more uncommon with present-day ABA.

Who practices Applied Behavior Analysis (ABA)?

- Different experts offer Applied Behavior Analysis (ABA). Projects ought to incorporate an accomplished ABA professional who manages the program, as well as the staff who work straightforwardly with your kid. These staffs are some of the time called conduct advisors or conduct interventionists.

- Professionals don't require formal capabilities to rehearse ABA treatment in Australia. Yet, there's a global certificate board - the Behavior Analyst Certification Board - which authorizes professionals as Board Certified Behavior Analysts. This license is generally utilized in the United States, however, it's not yet the public norm of authorization in Australia.

- It's smart to consider the capabilities and experience of any suppliers you're keen on.

- Educators, guardians, clinicians, and other unified wellbeing experts can all utilization ABA procedures and methodologies whenever they've been prepared by somebody with the suitable aptitude.

Where could you at any point track down an ABA specialist?

- Your GP or one of the different experts working with your kid can assist you with tracking down a supplier. You could likewise ask your NDIA organizer, youth accomplice, or neighborhood (LAC) if you have one.

- You can visit the Behavior Analyst Certification Board site to track down licensed professionals.

- Parent instruction, preparing, backing, and inclusion

- Assuming your kid is in an Applied Behavior Analysis (ABA) program, you'll assume a functioning part in your kid's program. You'll work with the ABA specialist to create and focus on your youngster's learning objectives. Frequently, ABA experts give parent preparing and backing to guardians, kin, and more distant family.

Cost contemplations

The expenses of ABA-based treatments and supports change contingent upon how long each week programs include, whether projects are balanced or bunch based, and how much management is involved.
You could remember the expense of involving ABA for kids' NDIS plans. You can contact the NDIS to find out.

Treatments and supports for Autism kids range from conduct treatments and formative ways to dealing with drugs and elective treatments. At the point when you comprehend the fundamental sorts of treatments and supports for Autism kids, it'll be simpler to figure out the methodology that will best suit your kid.

CHAPTER 7

The hidden potentials in Autistic kids

Autistic kids are many times solid in regions like visual, rule-based, and interest-based thinking.
A formative evaluation or an IQ test can distinguish Autistic youngsters' reasoning and learning qualities.
You can foster Autistic kids' abilities by working with their assets.

Thinking and learning qualities in Autistic kids
Autistic youngsters have numerous qualities and capacities. These may be qualities when contrasted and regularly creating youngsters, or individual qualities inside their ranges of abilities. When you resolve what your kid's assets and capacities are, you can utilize them to help your kid's turn of events.
The accompanying devices can assist you with more deeply studying your kid's reasoning and learning qualities:

Formative appraisal: this is utilized for youngsters as a feature of Autism conclusion. It estimates kids' assets in regions like non-verbal reasoning abilities, language and correspondence, and development.
Intelligence level test: this test estimates scholarly potential and capacities contrasted and youngsters of a similar age. It's utilized exclusively for youngsters matured four years and over.

Visual based abilities and Autism.
Visual reasoning can be a strength for Autistic kids. They may be great at visual hunt errands like tracking down a triangle inside a complicated picture or tracking down a red S in a bunch of red Xs and green Ss.
These solid visual abilities may be because medically introverted youngsters will quite often zero in on subtleties, as opposed to the entirety.
Likewise, medically introverted kids are many times visual students. This may be because visual data endures longer and is more concrete than spoken and heard data. It could assist Autistic youngsters with handling data and picking how to answer.

You can assist your kid with advancing by introducing data outwardly. You can likewise utilize your kid's visual abilities to help them in different regions. For instance:

Put visual updates around your home: If your kid can peruse, these can be composed words, however, they can likewise be pictures.
Take photographs of the different play exercises your kid can do, and put them on an 'action board' as an update or to assist your youngster with pursuing a decision.
Make photographs of the various strides engaged with day-to-day exercises, such as gathering a school pack or cleaning teeth. Stick the grouping on a wall close to where your youngster does every action.
Utilize visual backings for either the entire day or for day-to-day exercises.

Treatments and supports that utilize visual techniques frequently function admirably for medically introverted kids.

Rule-based thinking and Autism

Medically introverted youngsters are in many cases great at understanding and working with rules. You can utilize this solidarity to assist your kid with growing new abilities.

One method for doing this is by clarifying guidelines about the thing to do and when. This can make the 'covered up' rules of social collaboration and ordinary exercises more apparent, organized, and simple for your youngster to follow. For instance:

At the point when somebody comes to the entryway, make proper acquaintance.

At the point when it's sleep time, I clean my teeth.

Positive expressions like 'When x occurs, accomplish this ', work better compared to negative expressions like 'Don't '.

You could converse with different guardians or experts to get thoughts regarding what rules to incorporate.

It's likewise really smart to outwardly introduce rules. You could make a 'rule book' utilizing pictures and words. Peruse the 'rule book' to your youngster and let them take a gander at it at whatever point they need.

Decides that utilization 'on the off chance that' articulations can assist your kid with understanding what's happening around them, similar to how others are feeling. For instance, 'If Sam is chuckling, Sam may be cheerful'.

'If' articulations are additionally really great for exercises with clear advances and arrangements, so you can utilize them when you believe your kid should follow through with something. For instance, 'On the off chance that you put your shoes on, you can head outside. Or on the other hand, you can utilize a less difficult rendition - for instance, 'Shoes first, then outside'.

Exceptional subjects of interest and Autism

Autistic youngsters can frequently concentrate eagerly and gain some useful knowledge about things they're exceptionally intrigued by.

Here are a few thoughts for fostering your youngster's abilities by capitalizing on their exceptional advantages:

- **Play abilities:** when your kid is playing with their unique interest toys or protests, play close by them. You can grow your drop-in-the-bucket and interactive abilities by remarking on the thing you're both doing, trading toys, alternating, etc.
- **Numeracy abilities:** utilize your youngster's most loved toys to discuss varieties, numbers, and size - for instance, red toy vehicles and blue toy vehicles, huge trucks and little motorbikes, etc.
- **Everyday consideration abilities:** foster your kid's capacity to participate by incorporating their inclinations into testing exercises. For instance, if having a shower is testing, you could give your kid some unique interest toys to play with in the shower, or stick photos of your kid's exceptional subject around the shower as an idea.

- **Discussion abilities:** talk with your youngster about their unique advantages. This could give your kid additional inspiration to impart and chat with you. Your youngster could begin by giving a discourse as opposed to having a discussion. You could continuously present inquiries, and get your kid to ask you inquiries as well.
- As your kid progresses in years, you can search for ways of involving their extraordinary advantages in a single region to fabricate abilities in different regions. For instance, assuming that your kid has great PC abilities, they could jump at the chance to find out about coding or creating computer games. Or on the other hand, if your youngster loves Thomas the Tank Engine, they may be intrigued to find out about train networks in your space.

Repetition memory abilities and Autism

Autistic youngsters are much of the time great at advancing by heart (repetition memory). Numerous Autistic kids can recall enormous pieces of data, similar to discussions from motion pictures, words to a melody, number plates, etc.

You can urge your kid to involve repetition memory for learning helpful data, similar to your telephone number and address, the letter set, and times tables.

CHAPTER 8

Make out time to rest

Stress is a typical piece of life, however, families with medically introverted youngsters frequently have a great deal of pressure.

For stress, the executives, take a stab at setting aside a few minutes for family exercises, doing positive reasoning and unwinding works out, and getting coordinated and that's just the beginning.

On the off chance that you or other relatives feel extremely focused on each day, converse with well-being proficient like your GP.

About pressure in families with autistic youngsters

Stress is an ordinary piece of life, something that the vast majority and most families experience.

However, families with medically introverted kids can encounter more pressure than different families.

For instance, they could feel worried because they:

- are grappling with determination and how it affects their youngster
- are finding it hard to oversee day-to-day existence with a medically introverted youngster
- are experiencing difficulty overseeing testing conduct in their autistic youngster
- doesn't know how to assist their autistic kid with building certainty and a positive mental self-portrait

- need a break from really focusing on their autistic youngster yet don't have any idea how to get a reprieve
- are experiencing difficulty exploring the assistance framework.

Albeit autism determination influences the entire family, relatives may be focused on various things about the finding or various parts of existence with an autistic kid. They could likewise answer and express pressure in various ways.

Some pressure can be OK, giving you the inspiration and concentration to confront difficulties and finish things. Be that as it may, an excessive amount of pressure can be overpowering, making it challenging to adapt to ordinary things.

So assuming you feel your family is experiencing difficulty adapting, effectively dealing with the pressure in your day-to-day life is significant.

Stress can influence individual relatives, and it can likewise influence your associations with one another. Perceiving each other's sentiments and caring for your family connections can assist you with family stress the executives.

Diminishing and overseeing pressure for families with medically introverted youngsters

Although pressure is an ordinary piece of everyday life, a lot of pressure can make a negative difference. There are useful things you can do to deal with your family's pressure.

Overseeing pressure is great for the profound and emotional well-being and prosperity of everybody in your loved ones.

Positive reasoning and self-talk

Good reasoning and self-talk increment your good sentiments. Furthermore, feeling good expands your capacity to adapt to upsetting circumstances.

For instance, you could have a pessimistic idea like 'Individuals presumably believe I'm a terrible parent. You can challenge this idea by asking yourself, 'How do I have at least some idea that individuals will think this?' You could likewise utilize more certain contemplations, similar to 'Who tends to think about others' thought process?', 'I can do this, or 'I will remain even headed'.

The more you practice positive self-talk, the more programmed it will become in your life. Begin rehearsing in one circumstance that causes you stress, and afterward, continue toward another.

Unwinding and breathing techniques

Practice a few breathing activities and muscle unwinding procedures. If you practice and use unwinding practices when you feel indications of stress, or when you realize you're going into a circumstance that makes you push, it can quiet things down.

You could likewise save a tad of time every day for unwinding, reflection, or care. Indeed, even 10 minutes toward the start or day's end could be sufficient. This could help you rest better and feel better during the day.

Getting coordinated

Stress is in many cases connected with the inclination that things are beyond your control. Getting coordinated is an extremely viable method for fixing things - including your feelings of anxiety -.

For instance, if you have a rundown of things you want to do, you can deal with the rundown, zeroing in on only each thing in turn. What's more, you'll feel far better as you cross things off the rundown.

You could likewise take a stab at setting some family schedules in motion. Schedules assist your family with overcoming your errands all the more productively and save time for additional charming things. You can change these schedules for kids with extra necessities.

Setting aside a few minutes for pleasant family exercises

At the point when you have a medically introverted kid, you could neglect to set aside a few minutes for yourself. You can decrease the feelings of anxiety in your family by ensuring that all relatives - including you have the opportunity and willpower to do things that encourage them.

One method for doing this is by getting everybody in your family to make a rundown of things that they appreciate. Then attempt to ensure that everybody will accomplish something from their rundown consistently or each several days. The rundowns ought to have a blend of exercises that differ in cost and time.

Keeping up with and changing family customs and ceremonies

Family customs and ceremonies can provide you with a feeling of having a place and harmony. This can reinforce your family connections, which will assist you with traversing unpleasant times.

You could need to alter your practices to suit the requirements of your autistic kid. For instance, it may very well be less upsetting to design an end-of-the-week setting up camp outing somewhat nearer to home so you invest less energy in the vehicle.

Support from loved ones

At the point when a youngster gets autism determination, loved ones can be an incredible wellspring of functional help. It's great to request help assuming you want it. It very well may be as straightforward as asking a more distant family part to mind a couple of hours one evening or asking a more seasoned niece or nephew to take your kids to the recreation area. This could transform into a pleasant action for your kid and more distant family part, as well as allowing you to yourself or time to finish different things.

Rest

Rest care can offer you a reprieve from really focusing on your autistic kid and assist you with overseeing pressure. Assuming that you have a stressed outlook on leaving your kid with somebody outside the family, set aside a few minutes for break carers to get to know your kid before they care for your kid.

Finding support with pressure
On the off chance that you or some other relatives are feeling extremely focused on each day, it could assist with conversing with a wellbeing proficient person. You could begin by seeing your GP, who can assist you with arranging overseeing pressure. This could incorporate alluding you or other relatives to one more well-being proficient for some expert help.

Your family can likewise get support from the accompanying administrations:

Relief care - contact your state or domain Autism affiliation, or a Commonwealth Respite and Carelink Center.
NDIS support - contact the National Disability Insurance Scheme to learn about help to assist your youngster with arriving at their singular objectives and carrying on with the existence they need.
Support gatherings - contact neighborhood or online gatherings to associate with others in comparable circumstances.
Monetary help - contact Centrelink about carer stipend, carer installment, and other monetary help.
At the point when your pressure is taken care of and you're feeling great as a parent, you're better ready to explore the difficulties of everyday life. This assists your kids with developing, creating and flourish.

CHAPTER 9

Things to avoid when raising an autistic child

Raising a kid with Autism can be both testing and fulfilling.

1) Children with Autism don't convey, play, or act like their neurotypical peers, and their ways of behaving can be confounding, disappointing, or honestly disturbing to certain guardians or watchmen.
Simultaneously, kids with Autism have qualities and capacities that can arise when a parent is tuned in and ready to take part in a way that turns out best for their kid. This intends that, when you have a kid with Autism, it's not generally best to simply go with what feels normal to you as a parent or watchman.
You might have to change your nurturing style or normal inclinations to address a kid's issues. All in all, you might have to deliberately stay away from these nurturing styles that can rapidly subvert your relationship with a kid in Autism range.

Micro-manager Parenting
Micro-manager guardians drift over their youngsters, watching and responding to everything they might do. They jump in to help when an issue shows up not too far off; they mediate to smooth each way; they demand extraordinary treatment for their descendants.

Overly controlling nurturing is not great for any kid, as it makes autonomy and self-assurance particularly hard to accomplish.
Guardians or gatekeepers of youngsters with Autism are inclined to overly controlling nurturing because they stress that their kid with Autism will run into issues they can't determine — and that is completely conceivable.
In any case, assuming overprotective nurturing stunts the advancement of neurotypical youngsters, envision how it helps kids with Autism.

2)Unable to advance by perception and model, kids with Autism should learn through direct guidance and by really doing.
At the point when you step in to take care of their responsibilities, you're denying your kid the chance to comprehend what's required, experience the test of endeavoring, partake in the adventure of progress, or gain the information created through the course of disappointment.

Competitive Parenting
Any parent or watchman who's been important for a Mommy and Me bunch has a ton of familiarity with serious nurturing. Whose child potty prepared first? Said the main word? Is taking the most classes, figuring out how to move or sing, playing peewee soccer, or concentrating on Chinese?
At the point when you have a kid with Autism, it tends to be difficult to try not to feel that the kid in your consideration is by and large abandoned. Yet, when you become involved with serious nurturing, you are sure to foster a feeling that the kid

in your consideration isn't satisfactory and that you, as a parent, are likely to fault.

As you can envision, the result is an inclination that neither you nor the kid you are raising is sufficient. The effect of such sentiments on a youngster with Autism may not be self-evident, however, they are genuine.

Hands-Off (Free-Range) Parenting

A few guardians and gatekeepers accept that their kids ought to be permitted to follow their interests and interests without parental obstruction. That functions admirably for certain neurotypical youngsters who are independent, self-spurred, and anxious to interface with others. It's not, in any case, a generally excellent decision for a youngster with Autism. While each youngster unquestionably needs and merits "down" time, kids with Autism truly need ordinary, centered parental engagement.

3) That's because, by and large, kids with Autism need your assistance to effectively figure out how to imagine, mingle, banter, get clarification on pressing issues, and research the world.

Without someone else to assist them with building these basic abilities, kids with Autism can turn out to be progressively removed and self-centered — and less fit or envious of participating in the more extensive world. They'll likewise have less of an open door to expand on their assets and accomplish their true capacity.

Perfectionistt (Tiger) Parenting

Indeed, a few youngsters flourish with guardians who demand straight A's, top athletic execution, wonderful sentence structure, and optimal social graces. Those kids are probably not going to be medically introverted.

Kids with Autism, while they might have numerous qualities, may have an exceptionally difficult stretch with numerous neurotypical youth assumptions. Their verbal abilities might be compromised, so high grades and wonderful language may not be attainable. They might experience issues with actual coordination, making games especially extreme.

It's essential to have elevated standards, in any event, for a kid with handicaps, yet make those assumptions excessively high, and you and the kid in your consideration are in for unfortunate degrees of stress.

Tolerant Parenting

As the parent of a kid with Autism, you might feel that they ought to have no assumptions put about them beyond the everyday schedule. All things considered, it's extreme for mentally unbalanced children to work in school, and they merit a break.

You might try and feel it's preposterous to ask the kid in your consideration to finish family assignments, figure out how to quiet themselves, or control their way of behaving. The lamentable consequence of this sort of "do anything you desire" nurturing helps a kid to learn propensities and ways of behaving that will make difficult issues down the line.

Autism makes a few things more troublesome, yet in pretty much every case youngsters with Autism can do an extraordinary arrangement if they are asked and urged to do as such. At the point when you set the bar low, or deal with a kid with Autism with too little discipline, you are making it more challenging for them to comprehend or satisfy high hopes.

Understanding a youngster's difficulties is a certain something; expecting a kid to be inept is something else and hurtful.

Advantages of Rules and Discipline for Children With Autism

Excited Parenting

Since they got up earlier today, a preschooler with Autism has had five hours of social treatment, an hour each of discourse and exercise-based recuperation, two hours of parent-directed play treatment, and four hours of school.

When the kid falls into a depleted rest, you hop on the Internet to find one more helpful class, program, action, or asset to add to the timetable. With such a lot going on, the kid with Autism in your consideration has no open door to rehearse what they have realized, to meet and get to know another kid, or to just do what youngsters do (play).

As opposed to quickly looking for and participating in treatments and exercises, think about how conceivable it is that a couple of hours daily of quiet, unfocused parent or gatekeeper and youngster time may be only what a kid needs to develop and flourish.

No parent or watchman is awesome, and guardians or gatekeepers of youngsters with handicaps are feeling the squeeze more than most. A few guardians or watchmen may continually be overseeing serious conduct issues like medically introverted implosions, which can once in a while be startling.
That implies you might be more wrecked, drained, baffled, or restless than the typical parent or watchman, and have less monetary or profound assets to offer of real value.

While you're feeling overpowered, it's more than OK to connect for reprieve or backing, whether from other relatives and companions or from nearby associations that offer types of assistance to families with handicapped members.

4) Remember that focusing on yourself will permit you to help the kid in your consideration in the most ideal way.

www.ingramcontent.com/pod-product-compliance
Lightning Source LLC
LaVergne TN
LVHW050346160826
845677LV00014B/3821